Praise for

A Better December

"I've found it! The perfect gift for special friends at the season of the year that's so full of delights and stresses. This unique little gem of a book seems to have managed lightning strikes on every page—surprise lightning strikes of wit and wisdom that wouldn't let me put it down until I'd explored it to the end, an end that came all too soon. Steve, you've done it again—invented a new genre and made it soar."

> — **J. Robertson McQuilkin**, President Emeritus,
> Columbia International University

"In a uniquely original style, Steve seamlessly merges poetry, narration, and Scripture, with strikingly creative phrasing. A master of prose, poetry, and the Bible, Steve has written a little book that bends and blends genres. *A Better December* is a winning combo of insightful content about how to 'do life' (Steve's phrase) and innovative style. We enjoyed this little book so much that when we finished it, we immediately reread it—for its profound biblical tracing from Solomon to Someone, for its emphatic message about 'unstuffing' life, and for its fresh use of language and memorable style."

— **Don and Jenny Killgallon**, coauthors of the *Sentence-Composing* textbook series. Don teaches writing at the University of Maryland, Baltimore County

"Here's a book like you've never read before. It meets us at the intersection of ancient biblical wisdom and the dreams, struggles, and disappointments that are part of our Christmas season. With humor, poignancy, and clarity, Estes demonstrates that Solomon knew things about our holidays that we all need to know. With the help of Solomon, Estes shows you how you can have a Christmas that actually matches the message of the season you are celebrating."

— **Paul Tripp,** Paul Tripp Ministries; best-selling author

A BETTER DECEMBER

PROVERBS to BRIGHTEN CHRISTMAS

STEVEN ESTES

ILLUSTRATED BY SARAH BLAND HALULKO

Cover Photo and Design: Brandon Hill, bhilldesign.com
Typesetting and Interior Design: Faceout Studio

ISBN: 978-1-936768-67-7

Printed in Canada

20 19 18 17 16 15 14 13   2 3 4 5 6

To my children:

Ryan

Adrienne

Holly

Mark

Brock

Tyler

Clint

Dawson

Each of you, priceless

Foreword

Before you begin . . .

You know the feeling when you want to introduce your best friend to others? They're probably thinking, *Yeah, yeah, he's so special, what else is new?* But I simply cannot write this foreword without telling you about the man behind it.

When I was eighteen, I broke my neck in a diving accident and became paralyzed. Many people offered me comfort by quoting favorite Scriptures. But I was frightened of the Bible—it seemed antiquated and out of touch with my pain. Yet Steve made it winsome. With every page he turned there'd be a surprise. Something fresh and firsthand. He possessed the art of pulling those ancient words and placing them smack in the middle of everything current and contemporary. I was hooked.

He's done it again with *A Better December.* Flip to any page and Steve gives an arresting twist on our modern Decembers gone crazy.

Overspending and overeating. Too many Christmas sales, too many parties. Too many battles over manger scenes in the public square . . . and for some, too many sad memories from yesteryear.

Between the pages of this special little book, you'll find a genuine guide to the purposeful and peaceful holiday we all long for. Who'd ever have thought Proverbs would make a good Christmas read?! But it does. You're holding proof of it.

So let me introduce you to my best friend, Steve (well . . . my husband really holds that honor, but you know what I mean). And let him introduce you to Christmas the way it was meant to be celebrated!

JONI EARECKSON TADA

CONTENTS

Introduction

The longer I live, the more I like short books.

Here's one.

YESTERYEAR

About 3,000 years ago
the wisest man who ever lived
wrote a HUGE best seller.

A real wick-burner
about CHRISTMAS.

The funny thing is . . .
Christmas was still
1,000 years off.

His name was Solomon, king of Israel.

Here was one savvy author. A man who had unrolled a few scrolls in his day—who could handle himself with a quill. His market research nailed exactly what future readers would need come December.

C'mon, you say. Dusty ages ago, some guy was scratching on a sheepskin about hanging wool stockings over a fireplace?

Sure.

He knew about Bing Crosby? And parking lot jams on Black Friday?

Doubtless.

He foresaw my bloated VISA bill? Grasped the awkwardness of eye contact with those earnest bell-ringers standing by their red kettles? Knew about pine needles in my face when dragging in the tree?

Unquestionably.

Though I can understand your amazement.

After all . . .

. . . his family *was* Jewish. They weren't sure about a holiday that promotes plastic, plug-in reindeer on the front lawn.

His mother probably said,

"What's a nice Jewish boy
like you doing—
writing about Christmas?"

But Solomon forged ahead, sensing a definite trend on the horizon.
His blockbuster would be about:

Getting Through the Holidays

For as you know,
if there's one time of year
when things may not go
as planned . . .

. . . it's December.

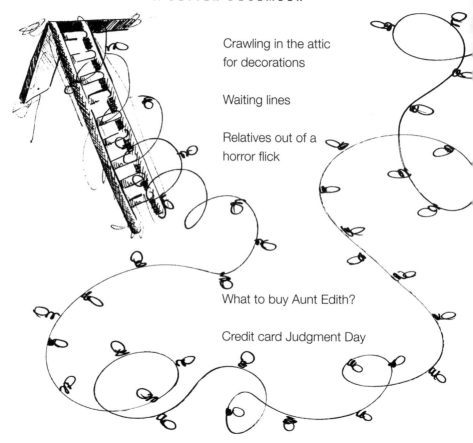

Crawling in the attic
for decorations

Waiting lines

Relatives out of a
horror flick

What to buy Aunt Edith?

Credit card Judgment Day

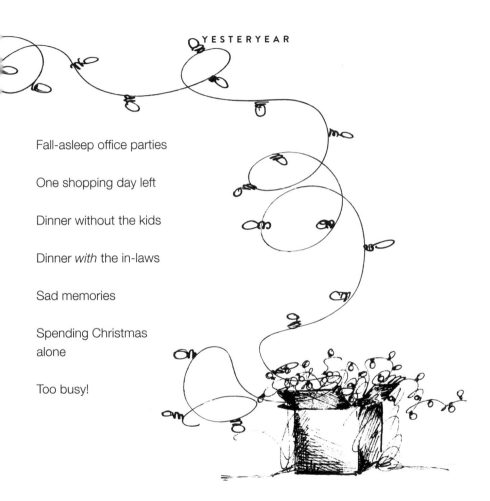

Fall-asleep office parties

One shopping day left

Dinner without the kids

Dinner *with* the in-laws

Sad memories

Spending Christmas
alone

Too busy!

Unreturnable "you-shouldn't-have" gifts

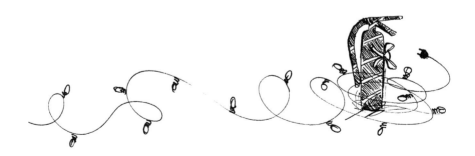

So, Solomon wrote his little book. (Good things come in small packages.)

He called it Proverbs. It's helpful in an everyday,
tie-your-shoes, commonsense way.

. . . and very Christmasy.

Not sure you can picture Solomon in a green and red sweater?

Think about it.

> Any writer who pens:
> "The coolness of snow . . .
> refreshes the spirit"
>> Proverbs 25:13

is all about December.

> Any poet with an eye for
> "an ornament of fine gold"
>> Proverbs 25:12

understands readers
willing to wrestle
an evergreen into the living room.

   Any author waxing lyrical that
   "Perfume and incense
   bring joy to the heart"

                Proverbs 27:9

would surely savor the whiff
of yuletide candles named
Spruce Forest or Vermont Sugar Cookie.

   And any man rolling his eyes about:
   "'It's no good, it's no good!'
   says the buyer—
   who then goes off and
   boasts about the purchase"

                Proverbs 20:14, author's paraphrase

feels for the cornered husband
held at fingernail point by his wife
'til she's finished recounting
her exploits in the mall.
Still not convinced?

Consider Solomon's little zinger below.
Tell me he never envisioned waking up to

pajama-clad urchins,
like Wee Three Kings,
avalanching down the stairs,
   bearing
      squeals
         giggles
           and whoopifications

WAY TOO EARLY

. . . on Christmas Day. Here's how he put it:

"If you shout a pleasant greeting
to your neighbor
too early in the morning,
it will be counted as a curse!"

Proverbs 27:14 NLT

You can bet your Macy's card, Solomon knows Christmas. He *gets* the stress of the year's twelfth month.

He shares his wisdom about it in Proverbs. The book in your hand sums up what he wrote.

Rummaging through these pages, you'll find he knows *your* Christmas.

He's practically been hiding
in your chimney.

GIFTS

Deep inside your head, voices whisper:

Your son will flunk science and his brain will atrophy into egg whites unless he gets the Every Kid's Quasar Wave Radio Telescope for his bedroom, scanning for life on other planets—"able to hear a pin drop from six billion light years."

Or . . .

Your daughter will consider you a goddess IF you can snag her the same boots worn by lead-singer Venus of the stage-rattling female rock band, the Deep Fried Voodoo Dolls.

Or . . .

Hari-kari is your only option, sir, short of receiving platinum-plated golf clubs—grip-fitted with a

material developed for Navy SEAL gloves when scaling sheer ice cliffs . . .
ropeless . . . in gale-force winds.

Or . . .

You, madame, will be caroled by angels and swept to Paradise
on gusts of rapture surpassing both LOVE and
CHOCOLATE when you open a gift box containing

. . . (you get the idea).

But Solomon, the world's richest
(not just wisest) man, said:

> "Death and Destruction
> are never satisfied,
> and neither are
> the eyes of man."

Proverbs 27:20

He's talking about your horde of THINGS that will soon feel *so* last-year.
They'll disappoint like the perfect week at the beach turned rain-soggy.

The day funeral homes close shop and hospitals sit empty, the day all
hurricanes are stillborn and death cries "Uncle!"—not 'til then, says Proverbs,
will your "eyes," your heart, be content with STUFF.

So the little book urges this prayer:

"Two things I ask of you,
O Lord . . . ,
give me neither poverty
nor riches,
but give me only my daily bread.
Otherwise, I may have too much
and disown you . . .
Or I may become poor and steal."

Proverbs 30:7–9

Go ahead and prowl the mall,
he's saying—
shop the net,
wrap a few gifts,
pencil a wish list yourself.

But keep it simple,
and remember
what's important.

"Neither poverty nor riches" under the tree.

It'll work better that way.

Really.

CONTENTMENT

What? *Starting* to write checks for that easy chair
only after the dog chews it ragged, Uncle Ralph
sloshes eggnog over it, and your enthusiasm
has flown south with the snow birds?
Silly. But Solomon's raised eyebrow
about impulse-buying goes deeper
than rescuing us from featherbrained
decisions about money:

> "The unfaithful are trapped
> by evil desires."
>
> Proverbs 11:6

17

Evil desires? Unfaithful? Sounds like the Grinch plotting to ruin Christmas in Who-ville—not a shopper who's a sucker for a sales pitch. Surely a few dreams about flopping onto soft cushions aren't so sinister?

But Proverbs says, "They might be" if:

> . . . I'm "trapped" by this chair,
> not just sitting on it.

> . . . my debt keeps rising
> as my resolve keeps melting.

> . . . I care more for a La-Z-Boy
> than for my wife who gulps at the sticker price.

Don't think Solomon's rapping your knuckles. He's pointing the way to a peaceful house:

"Better a little
with the fear of the Lord
than great wealth
with turmoil."

Proverbs 15:16

That is:

What good is a spiffy living-room recliner if it doubles as your mattress because your wife has barricaded the bedroom door?

Far better to have a house where the upholstery is frayed but the relationships are smooth.

CHILDREN

Once upon a time . . . no, really . . . this happened. In a family with kids.

Kids? someone asks. Were they like mine? Sweet little elves whom December sometimes turns impish? Did they act up waiting in line for a handshake with Santa? Whine in the restaurant 'til Mom and Dad blushed like poinsettias?

Just wait. It wasn't that simple.

Once upon a time, outside a department store, a boy sat on the sidewalk—all of three years old. Chubby-fingered and solid as a sandbag. Next to him sat his sister, wispy haired and bird legged, a little slip of a thing—but older and wiser at age five.

A stone's throw away, a woman kept a watchful eye on them while trundling a shopping cart back to its place. Their grandmom. I knew these kids. I knew this lady . . . well loved by all. Wise as an owl, practical as oatmeal.

The boy sat elbows-on-knees, chin in his palms, serving his sentence: hard time on the curb for crimes committed. I can't recall the exact offense—accounts vary. It happened long ago, and the court records have gone up in smoke. But knowing this judge, I can guess the charges: criminal fussing, felony back talk, or perhaps aggravated toy grabbing while riding in a cart in a retail establishment.

Keep your eye on the sister. Beside the boy. Our lady of perpetual consolation. She wraps an arm around him.

"It's okay, Marky."

Then, not one for words without deeds, she adds, "Here, you can have this." She reaches with her other hand and puts something in his mouth, something soothing to his young palate.

Slurp, slurp, slurp. Life's not so bad.

Grandmom returns, comes upon the scene: sister offering her silent ministrations—left hand patting her brother's back; right hand . . . thumb in his mouth.

*   *   *

Cheers for big sister.

But what about that awful grandmother? What's with this heavy-handed justice? This squelching of aspirations? This quenching of the human spirit?

On behalf of this woman, Solomon would offer his own thumb—pointed upward in approval. For in Proverbs, he cringed at the notion that any authority figure, including a parent or grandparent, should care only that a good time is had by all:

> "If a man pampers his servant
> from youth, he will bring
> grief in the end."
>
> Proverbs 29:21

December's pressures can besiege Mom and Dad into saying, "Aw, heck, I'm too tired to make them behave." Into throwing up their hands—removing the mold from the kids before the Jell-O has set.

You want folks to *respect* your son, to *like* your daughter. You hope for the little sprigs to swell you with pride someday. But getting there needs to start now . . . even on Christmas morning.

Picture a boy on the Big Day, primed and wide-eyed beside the tree. A scene worthy of a Hallmark Cards commercial. But watch. He doesn't just open his presents—he cannon-balls into the pile:

Eating through gifts
like a wood chipper.
Ripping open boxes
like the Jaws of Life.

No word of thanks.
No hug of gratitude.
No shred of restraint.

Just a bored shrug: "Is this *all*?"

Who will help this boy?

Maybe Dad? But he's hands-off with the kids, dreaming about escape to the garage or impatiently fingering the TV remote.

Maybe Mom? She's wiped out from being mom *and* dad, weary of playing the heavy.

How about the grandparents? No, they're smiling and nodding: "He's only young once—let him be a boy."

But a little correction today will send you bonus checks for decades.

> "Train a child in the way he should go,
> and when he is old
> he will not turn from it."
>
> Proverbs 22:6

And if your much-loved bundle of consumerism throws a fit?

> "Do not withhold discipline
> from a child."
>
> Proverbs 23:13

"[The indulgent parent] hates his son,
but he who loves him
is careful to discipline him."

Proverbs 13:24

An out-of-control child will enjoy Christmas Day MORE under a kind but firm hand, after

a stint in the corner,
a good cry,
and a reassuring hug.

(Otherwise, it's runny Jell-O everywhere.)

PERFECTIONISM

When my wife was little, her family was Amish. Barn raisings, buggies, high-stepping horses, shoofly pies—the whole postcard.

Later, they left that life and became mainstream farmers. The suspenders and bonnets were gone, but they remained hard-working, no nonsense, sweep-the-porch folks. As good-natured a family as homemade jam and bread.

I grew up taking in the city. Mom and I would hop the streetcar into downtown Baltimore. Lights, crowds, noise, action—the busier, the better. Birthdays were a big thing, Christmas, bigger yet. Whoop it up. Break some eggs, make an omelet.

My wife and I met in college. I first saw Verna from across the cafeteria. Popular as a lemonade stand in summer. Prettier than an evening meadow blinking with fireflies. I was hooked. Proposed on the beach. We walked the aisle, started life together.

Verna kept everything worthwhile from her childhood and folded the rest into a drawer. Worked circles around any woman you'd know. Line dried the wash, taught the kids, pinched the pennies. Joined me in whatever hoopla I wanted, but—in her mother's meat-and-potatoes tradition—NEVER got exotic in the kitchen.

. . . until one December.

Wishing to please—wanting some memories for the kids—she found a recipe book. Brimming with color photos. Promises of the perfect Christmas. The kind, no doubt, her husband recalled from urban days of yore.

PERFECTIONISM

Sugar plums in her head, practical impulses stuffed away in an apron pocket, she purchased the ingredients to yuletide bliss. A concoction to bless the family forever.

The evening has arrived. The fortunate are assembled about the table. There is to be a holiday surprise:

"Festive Yule Log."

Candles aglow, faces upturned. The platter of glory is borne to the table. Mother seated. Nod given.

Trembling forks sink into the first sampling mouthful. Eyes closed for concentration. The pregnant pause. . . . A searching for words. The furtive glances. The first stifled chortle. Then,

Oh, the hooting and howling.
The slappings on the table.
The witticisms.
The criticisms.

Centered on the table, the Yule Log sulks—rolled in a fine gravel posing as crushed nuts. A taste akin to cream cheese blended with toothpaste— perhaps Crest, no, Colgate. As if sautéed in soy sauce, glued into shape by an application of Crisco. The look of a food item suspected of disease, held in quarantine at Customs.

Verna smiles weakly. Rises. Whisks the mistake into exile. All the while carols from the record player begin straying off-key . . . and Misters Currier & Ives are ushered to the backyard, blindfolded, and shot.

* * *

Solomon foresaw that many designs for Christmas Eve would go awry. Why else would he write:

> "Do not boast about tomorrow,
> for you do not know
> what a day may bring forth"?
>
> Proverbs 27:1

Or . . .

"You can make many plans,
but the Lord's purpose
will prevail"?

Proverbs 19:21 NLT

God has bigger plans for you than the perfect dinner. That's why he lets
things go wrong. He's saving your appetite for the perfect *eternity*. He notices
you smitten with this short life,

feeling it slip through your fingers,
trying to shake a snow-globe Christmas
out of every December.

The *true* holiday magic is reserved for heaven. Every delight down here is a
mere taste and teaser.

Knowing that, doesn't it ease the pressure just a bit as you flip through recipes
on the 24th—biting your lip . . . pondering a go at that Festive Yule Log?

(by the way, Verna recovered nicely)

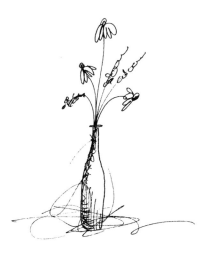

SURPRISES

Out of the toasty car,
into the see-your-breath night,
silent as orphan stars,
the family slips.

Keeping to the shadows,
creeping through the neighborhood.
What would be the likelihood?!
One of them trips!

"Oooh! Ouch! Jeepers!"

Shhh!

Bundled to the eyebrows,
resolute as snowploughs,

festive as the shiny boughs
of holly in a hall.

Over someone's frozen yard,
up the splintery stairs.
Do we have the right address?
(Check the slip of paper.)

Yes.

Set the box down,
full of goodies—
sweets and toys
and frozen chickens.

Will this score well?
Hit the doorbell!
(running like the dickens)*

* Editor's note: Literary critics detect here an allusion to the author of *A Christmas Carol*.

Father, mother, sister, brother,
crouching in the bushes . . .

(whispering and shushes).

Porch light on.
Head sticks out.
Head looks down.
Head looks about.

Calls out a name.
Footsteps on the floor.
A second head now.
And then several more.

. . . standing in their socks.
. . . looking in their box.

Two families huddled
outside in the night,
one by the front door,
one out of sight.

One has been hungry,
one's been worthwhiling.
Both families full now,

. . . both of them smiling.

* * *

Somebody in this poem has been taking Solomon's advice:

"He who is kind to the poor
lends to the Lord,
and he will reward him
for what he has done."

Proverbs 19:17

And . . .

"He who refreshes others
will himself be refreshed."

Proverbs 11:25

Such a deal! You're strapped for cash this time of year. Frazzled. Or dreading
the in-laws. But as you forget yourself and remember others with even
emptier pockets and truly dismal lives—God will knock at YOUR life's door
with boxes of his own.

OTHERS

That divorced guy next door—whose wife grabbed the kids and sped off? Maybe he deserved it; maybe he didn't. But no bowl of holiday punch can dull his pain this season.

For . . .

> "Heartache crushes the spirit."
>
> Proverbs 15:13

and . . .

> "A crushed spirit who can bear?"
>
> Proverbs 18:14

He needs a family. Maybe *yours*. Why not kindle a little hope? Christmas dinner, a small gift, human warmth.

What's that?
Your dinner won't be much—
as meager as Bob Cratchit's?

To that man, it will taste like a prize turkey.

"He who is full loathes honey,
but to the hungry
even what is bitter
tastes sweet."

Proverbs 27:7

"Better a meal of vegetables
where there is love
than a fatted calf with hatred."

Proverbs 15:17

And you'll feel like the renewed
Mr. Scrooge who had that turkey
delivered after his three-ghost night.

OTHERS

* * *

Those new folks across the street—the flatlanders from Iowa? Sure they smile and wave. But guaranteed, your quaint New England hills give them claustrophobia like a mall on Black Friday.

They're not dazzled by your Red Sox. They're thinking home. The rustle of corn. Endless horizon. Relatives who don't say CLEE-ugh when singing *It Came Upon a Midnight CLEAR.*

But all that is far away. The last plains they saw were in a rearview mirror. These people need you. Borrowed family. Especially on holidays, when things get lonely.

> "Better a neighbor nearby
> than a brother far away."
>
> Proverbs 27:10

* * *

Know a relief worker far from home? A college kid in some cheerless dorm? A soldier with foreign sand blowing onto his holiday turkey? Some well-chosen words from you might do wonders. And *your* mailbox is liable to light up in return. For Solomon says:

> "Like cold water to a weary soul
> is good news from a distant land."
>
> Proverbs 25:25

> "Pleasant words are a honeycomb,
> sweet to the soul."
>
> Proverbs 16:24

LONGINGS

Deep last night we tramped through our forest. (Deep comes early this time of year.) Under a squirrel's hole, over the snow crust, down our dirt lane—just for the sake of it.

. . . four of my sons and me.

Talked as we walked. Nothing important. Crested the hill—the wind drew its knife. Thrust our bare noses through weather we live for: twelve degrees Fahrenheit . . . whimpering toward zero.

Home again, downstairs, stamping and sniffling. Coats on pegs, rubbing our hands. Age 16 hoists a log from the stack, a hardwood we felled . . . an oak we remember. It had a knot (we recall), mocked our axe.

But we had grabbed a wedge and a sledge, and that was that. Five guys bend to peer in a wood stove—witnesses to justice, glad to see it burn.

"Time for tunes!" says Age 24. "Yep, let's do it," says Age 19. So deep last night we tramped down the hall. To 24's bedroom, a place we could crash.

. . . four of my sons and me.

More a studio than a bedroom. Bunk elbowed into a corner. Microphones duck-taped to a forest of stands. Wires askew like a girl's hair in a wind storm. Scrunched. I flop on a mattress to listen. Guys grabbing guitars. The eldest, ensconced behind snares and cymbals—a ship's captain on the bridge. He twirls a drumstick to get its feel. Next summer, marriage. This Monday, back to college. But tonight . . . the guys. Lumberjacks fingering frets. I aim a camera, capture their silhouettes.

. . . four of my sons and me.

Like a quick-melting icicle, the sound of light plinking on a cymbal. It cascades into an intro, and they start to lay it down. Smooth as poured coffee, the bass eases in. Sap rises in the stands, each microphone buds. Clever lyrics, catchy riffs. Young men, heads nodding with the easy magic. Not perfect . . . yet perfect.

. . . four of my sons and me.

Three songs into the set, the eldest speaks. "Hey, Dad, wanna sit in?" Grinning from his drum stool, he offers me the sticks. Because he loves me . . . and for the comedy. The pleasure of seeing an orangutan beat a trash can.

We laugh. They know I'm a schmoe on the cow bell and snare. But these boys don't know everything:

I am young, fit, happening. Can feel the heft of my twelve-string—knowing in a moment it will surge into life. We take the stage. Approach the mics.

Relaxed but excited. Five best friends—three guys, two girls. A university gig. (In our minds we're The Mamas and the Papas). Voices blending. Lives mingling. Ready smiles. Easy laughter. And really, really cool bell bottoms. A hundred years ago . . .

. . . four of my friends and me.

My sons know this—the way they know that $E=mc^2$ or that Helsinki is the capital of Finland. It may be true, but so what? Now is now. Dad is a black and white photo. They've watched for twenty-plus years as pastoring a church has sucked most of my oxygen. They see my fingers forgetting their skill—as their hands coax pleasing sounds from high on the necks of their instruments.

But how could they grasp my view from that basement bed? The delight, the loss? The sense of sons passing me in a blur? How could they know I was fingering invisible chords as they played? That earlier, outside on the lane, my wayworn knees could barely keep pace? That I love their world but glimpse it only from the edges?

So, this final weekend of Christmas break, I answer my eldest as he offers the drumsticks.

"No, thanks. You go ahead."

"Okay, Pops." He does. They do.

   . . . four of my sons.

* * *

Solomon pictured such evenings three millennia ago:

"Even in laughter the heart may ache."

Proverbs 14:13

What warms the soul, he noted, can sadden it. Especially during the holidays. The jingling of bells, the blazoning of brass, the chorusing of carols—delighting one listener—bend another low, as if under sleet.

"Like one who takes away a garment on a cold day, . . .
is one who sings songs
to a heavy heart."

Proverbs 25:20

What better month than December to be in love! What worse time of year for romance to pass by, or grow dim in memory—as in this poem by Yeats, near his life's end, penned shortly before the Second World War:

> How can I, that girl standing there,
> My attention fix
> On Roman or on Russian
> Or on Spanish politics . . .
> But O that I were young again
> And held her in my arms.

Polar winds of sorrow can chill the soul in family-filled, memory-laced December:

> the chair now empty
>
> the daughter now just a photo
>
> the ring returned
>
> (or never received)

words blurted hastily

(or never ventured)

the longing for childhood

the home left behind

Solomon annotates life's bittersweet journey with piercing simplicity:

"Each heart knows its own bitterness,
and no one else can share its joy."

Proverbs 14:10

Ultimately, he says, you're alone with your thoughts. No spouse, child, parent, friend, or lover knows exactly what you feel as you stroll the corridor of life.

Especially at Christmas.

. . . Some help, please, Solomon.

DISAPPOINTMENT

Okay, so Solomon's lamp sheds light on the problems of Christmas. He boxes his insights in pithy sayings. Wraps them in colorful words. Ties them with bows of poetry.

Proverbs charcoals a sketch about holiday office parties—mocking the workplace clown, the

"fool who is full of food"

Proverbs 30:22

. . . making us grin.

The quick-witted king stuffs your stocking with tips for life. Words to the wise. He's all about facing down December and its woes.

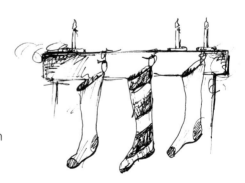

"Here's the recipe," he counsels,

Pour yourself a bowlful of wisdom.
Sprinkle in a dash of self-restraint.
Add a mug's worth of love for the empty, the hurting.
Grab a wooden spoon and (after waving a warning to little Marky) stir in some family outreach.
Lower expectations to 350° for thirty minutes in the kitchen of your soul.

And voila!

CHRISTMAS CONTENTMENT!

. . . sort of.

But why am I still empty? . . .

Solomon waxes eloquent about self-discipline. Yet wasn't he the guy
with 300 wives
and more concubines
than snowflakes in a blizzard?

The famous sage warns against the lure of *things,* the siren call of *stuff.* Yet concerning God's temple we read:

> "[Solomon] spent
> seven years building it,"
>
> 1 Kings 6:38

whereas,

> "It took Solomon thirteen years,
> however, to complete the construction
> of his [own] palace."
>
> 1 Kings 7:1

The author of Proverbs urges our affections heavenward. Yet didn't material gods of wood and stone finally trip Solomon's own feet, and ruin his life? (see 1 Kings 11:1–12)

Didn't he place his confidence in
horses and chariots
against God's express command?

WHAT'S GOING ON HERE?

Here's what.

Every word of Proverbs is
faithful as an old dog,
solid as that oaken log,
crackling in your fireplace.

God's very words (Proverbs)
were funneled to struggling people (us),
through a gifted author (Solomon).

BUT . . . in the end, Israel's wise king couldn't heed his own counsel—or do
life any better than you.

This Christmas, you need more than good advice (even divine advice). You need HELP.

Pulling you from the snowbank of "me, always me."

Stoking in you the want to give a hoot about others.

A hand when you've slipped on life's ice and can't get up.

Someone to fix what you've broken. Who loves you anyway. Who reads your soul—though you're a mystery to yourself, like a book unwritten.

You need comfort in the solitary hours of the year's shortest days and longest nights.

You need . . .

. . . someone much better than Solomon.

SOMEONE

At age seventeen, in the sweltering cotton fields a stone's throw from Old Man River, Charlie one day straightened his back, threw down his hoe, hollered he'd had enough, marched the dirt miles to the recruiter's office, lied about his age, and took his ticket to see the world: the U.S. Coast Guard. Later, after the war, the U.S. Merchant Marine.

In ports the planet over, Charlie dragged his buddies out of bars, up the gangway, back onto the ship. Everybody's great guy. No bottle ever called to him—he'd seen in Tennessee what alcohol did to men. But Charlie had other tastes he could never quite shake—soft hair, soft voices, thin waists.

Now, In his early thirties, a landlubber's life. Wife, two small kids—boredom, angst, guilt. Rattling across Baltimore, alone in his tired electrical truck. Two blocks from nondescript Dolefield Avenue.

Past a laundromat and similar thrills.

"God, I'm not even sure you exist," he heard himself say. Big topic for a guy running copper wire for a living. Light red. Light green. What's the difference? "If you do, I don't know if you're listening." Horns, traffic. Charlie oblivious. Tired of Charlie.

He remembered his sailing days. Gibralter. Sicily. India. Religions everywhere. "Are the Hindus right?" (Was he up to this?) "If so, I'll ship out first chance and head for the Pacific." (What's to lose?)

He thought of religious types he'd met here in the States. Liberals, Bible thumpers, crystal wavers, the gamut. Some of them interesting, even impressive. Some off their rocker. "If the Jews have it right, I'll see the rabbi in the synagogue off Pratt Street." (A little peace should be worth wearing a yarmulke.) "The Christians? I'll join a church." Drumming his fingers. "The Jehovah's Witnesses? I'll find a Kingdom Hall and knock on doors."

(So forth and so on.)

Bus fumes. Gears shifting. Nothing.

"But I need you . . ."

Dolefield Avenue, two hundred feet ahead. Hitting the blinker.

"Whatever your name . . ."

Dolefield, under his front bumper.

"Whoever you are . . . (hopeless) . . . I'm asking, . . .
take over."

Into the intersection. Making the left. A speck in a truck in a city of a million.
But before the steering wheel straightened . . . or the blinker stopped . . .
Charlie *knew* who was listening.

He forgot India. Dropped Pratt Street. Dismissed Kingdom Hall. Unable to
drive, he pulled to the curb, killed the engine, and wept for twenty minutes in
the presence of Jesus of Nazareth.

* * *

Charlie had met a *person.* Not a book about a person, or a gifted author's excellent suggestions, but *someone* who repeatedly invited discouraged people to . . .

Come.
Come.
Come.
Come.

COME ...

Come.
Come . . .
Come . . .

(Matthew 11:28; 14:29; 19:21; Mark
1:17; Luke 14:17; 18:16; 19:5;
John 1:39; 7:37; 21:12; and others)

When they came, here's what happened:

To a spoiled rich kid:

> "Jesus looked at him and loved him."
>
> Mark 10:21

To Peter, drowning in Lake Galilee:

> "Immediately Jesus reached out
> his hand and caught him."
>
> Matthew 14:31

To favor-seekers crowding the doorway—limping, dripping disease, schlepping emotional baggage:

> "He had compassion on them, because they were harassed and helpless, like sheep without a shepherd."
>
> Matthew 9:36

Was Charlie's soul, so mysterious to himself, just a blank space on the divine cartographer's map?

> "Jesus knew their thoughts."
>
> Luke 11:17

Would his sins keep the crucified healer forever distant?

> "When Jesus rose . . . , he appeared first to Mary Magdalene, out of whom he had driven seven demons."
>
> Mark 16:9

Could a man so prone to melancholy, especially every Christmas, ever taste joy?

"Blessed are you who weep now, for you will laugh."
Luke 6:21

As for the years that followed: modest earnings all his life; faithful to his wife and kids. True to his word, they joined a church. Year after year, seven days a week, morning and evening they read the Bible together and, usually on their knees, prayed.

Nights and weekends he started helping whom he could: under someone's car hood, in somebody's hospital room, driving a widow somewhere. Mornings at five saw him in his green stuffed chair, reading through the Bible yearly, making good on an eighth-grade education.

Not a perfect man. Watching his soul slowly getting sanded along the grain. The sawdust getting smaller.

Spent his last years walking (shuffling, really) Baltimore's toughest sidewalks—approaching bums, befriending addicts, chauffeuring the homeless. Mind still sharp, but the body of a rusty Ford—something always breaking. A gray-haired dinosaur posing a threat to no one so that hard, unlikely men would stop and listen . . . be listened to . . . learn about someone Charlie had met years ago on Dolefield Avenue.

By age sixty-four he was gone. The funeral line snaked forever. Among the mourners, some homeless guys—a few now sober, employed . . . married . . . forgiven.

They learned at the service how Charlie had refused most medication in his last weeks. Not to be stubborn, not to be a hero. But to be awake when the time came.

"I'd like my head clear on that day," he confided to his family. "And if possible, I've asked the Lord if he'd let me feel pain when it comes."

"Why?"

"For the closeness," he said. "He's always been the closest when I've physically suffered the most. I'd like to experience him with me when I go."

Your Christmas is hard, your December difficult. Nothing tastes. Joy has moved on. But a Norman Rockwell holiday that recreates yesteryear is not the answer. Nor is it a charge-card binge, or even your son coming home. The answer is Jesus. Changing you, forgiving you, *in* you—whether he is a gift you've never opened or has been your Savior since childhood but you rarely phone anymore.

Fifteen minutes after I left his bedroom, his hands on the shoulders of a pair of tearful visitors whom he loved, praying aloud that they would find Jesus, Charlie died. Of another heart attack . . . in great pain.

I, too, have a melancholy nature. I long for things at Christmas I can't put my finger on. But even in December, I'm okay. I'm okay from knowing Jesus. I met him through a man who year after year, seven days a week, morning and evening, read the Bible to my sister and me from his green stuffed chair.

CHANGES

It's not just *your* Christmas that will change when you know Jesus.

Smack in the middle of age eleven, Josiah heard it on a Friday. You have leukemia. Which led to the children's hospital and tests leading to marrow transplants and spinal-tap headaches and one-to-three hours each way after work for Dad depending on traffic and chemo plus radiation equals nausea for months in the planet's most sterile room cuz you'll die if you leave it and Mom curled up on the chair at nights beside a hundred stuffed pandas piled to the ceiling . . .

Which was a double breath-taker because . . .

Smack in the middle of not-long-before, Josiah's mom heard it on a Tuesday. You have breast cancer. Which led to forms to sign and waiting rooms and surgery and pain but we didn't get it all so thirty days' radiation and a poorly healing wound needing five sew-ups in as many months and pain

then a second implant but it
appears your body's rejecting it
plus awful scar-pain so let's try
again we'll create a breast from
your stomach muscles (you'll need
narcotics for weeks for the pain) but postpone that
because we realize you have a child moving home
from another hospital . . .

Naturally, someone decided it was time to reach out.
So a family got together two big boxes of sodas, nuts,
fruit, plus snacks delightfully bad for you, and piled
into a van. Snow-blocked from parking too close,
they traipsed a hundred yards through slush, rang the
doorbell, and blurted Merry Christmas.

Pardon . . . I just realized. Are you perhaps
thinking it was *Josiah's* family who heard the
bell and answered the door? Good grief,
am I writing that poorly? His family *rang* the
bell, my wife's and mine, just weeks ago—

bearing gifts they traverse afar, grinning shyly like a farmer presenting flowers on a first date. They filled the doorway: Dad, Mom (between surgeries), and a clothesline-full of offspring, including Josiah—bald as a bowling pin under his hat, but with a hopeful thumbs-up from doctors.

Their presence said: You're our pastor; we appreciate you and Verna; why *wouldn't* we drop by with a little something? Typical of them. Mom, of course, had been sidelined of late from her endless kindnesses to others. But all along Dad and Josiah's brothers kept turning up for Car-Care Saturdays, serving widows and single moms at church—in-between zipping to the hospital.

Like I said . . . not just *your* Christmas will change if you know Jesus.

* * *

For those realizing that Solomon slipped off the bus, unnoticed, about ten stops ago, I wouldn't worry. He didn't mind being upstaged. As we speak, he's strolling grounds in heaven that dazzle even him.

"Heaven, even after all those foreign gods and extra wives?" you ask. Amazing, isn't it, whom God allows to repent?

Pardon the analogy, but forgiveness in bygone Solomon's day was like Christmas shopping with a credit card today. Take it home now, pay for it later.

In Solomon's case . . . a thousand years later. His crushing bill remained outstanding until the day one of his descendants stood before Pilate and with his silence asked for the tab.

The Man did this for Solomon. He did it for Josiahs and Charlies the world over. For the author of this book. For readers of this page.

A Man whose birthday always falls on Christmas . . .

Who said more than anyone realized, and told the plain-wrapper truth, when he pointed to himself before a needy crowd and announced:

"Someone greater than
Solomon is here."

Luke 11:31 NLT

LIGHT

What Exactly Happened on Dolefield Avenue?

Christmas in April. Night-become-day. An electrician rewired. Rebirth.

In his years as a sailor, Charlie had ambled past the display windows of many faiths: major world religions, offbeat groups, everything. Somewhere, he had obviously stumbled across the Christian gospel: the account of a Galilean peasant who raised a glass with the lowly yet spoke of the Almighty as if the two shared closet space. Who felt confident pardoning sins on his own authority. Who spent his last hours skewered to a Roman cross—but promised to rise again and make death hoist a white flag.

All these faiths were a blur to Charlie. But no matter; he wasn't a buyer. As a younger man, he considered his life well stocked. Had no nose for a bargain.

Yet in that electrical truck, as he called to "Whoever you are"—as he turned the corner and blurted, "Take over"—the only One who could actually hear him . . . did. Whatever scraps he knew about Jesus of Nazareth now did their work. Jesus poured the willingness to believe straight into his soul. Sweet eggnog into a glass. Like millions before him, Charlie found the pull irresistible and overwhelming. The guilt-ridden ex-seaman begged forgiveness for his strayings, surrendered to the man who had walked (not just sailed) on water, and was PARDONED and CHANGED.

Thus the Carpenter's words came true: "Here I am!" said Jesus. "I stand at the door and knock. If anyone hears my voice and opens the door, I will come in and eat with him, and he with me" (Revelation 3:20).

Hmm . . . Maybe you're in a truck, turning some corner in life. Maybe you should blurt out words to Someone from Nazareth.

A caution. Not everyone's first connection with Jesus will feel the same. For some, it's all wonder and dazzle: a thousand Christmas trees suddenly plugged in and sparkling. For others, it's gradual and quiet, as in the carol: "How silently, how silently, the wondrous gift is given."

What of Hindus, Jewish People, and Jehovah's Witnesses?

Upon believing in Jesus, Charlie left behind the views of other religions . . .
but not the *people* of those religions. He and a Jewish buddy regularly shared
rides to enjoy each other's company. One of the tearful visitors Charlie hugged
and prayed for aloud as he died was a Jehovah's Witness. At the funeral, an
expatriate from India confided to Charlie's wife, "He was the only real friend I
ever had."

If you are of another religion and your Christian acquaintances don't love
you—you have reason to doubt their Christianity. If they never risk speaking
with you about Jesus, who they believe holds the key to your eternal good—
you have reason to doubt their love.

Where Can I Meet Charlies and Josiahs?

Find a church . . . but not just any church. Not a morgue with a steeple. Not
a church with well-maintained buildings but no high-maintenance people.
Nor one primarily about the music (Bach *or* rock), or feel-good sermons (pop
psychology baptized with a hymn), or THE PASTOR, or Shakespeare, or
politics (left or right), or how all religions are really the same. Which is to say,
not a church where Jesus is shuffled to the back pew.

And certainly not one that worships a marshmallow Jesus—an everyone-play-nicely Jesus whose cross has been, as it were, scrubbed of its blood.

Rather, find a church that savors his death for us like hard candy on the tongue. One that ranks the Bible in importance with, say, air to breathe. Where they pray as if he's really listening. A church that enjoys all races and has time for complicated people. A church that embraces the poor and takes care of widows. Rub shoulders in a church like that (high church, low church, doesn't matter) and, although it won't be perfect, you'll meet Charlies and Josiahs. More importantly, you'll meet Jesus there nine Sundays out of ten.

But Jesus Makes Me Feel Guilty

Picture the world as divided between rule-breakers and rule-keepers. If you're the first, you avoid Jesus, saying, "Isn't he making a list and checking it twice? Gonna find out . . . (about everything unprintable that I've done)?"

In contrast, rule-*keepers* tend to imagine themselves as tighter with him than swaddling clothes on a baby. But obeying all those Commandments gets wearisome, and truth be told, the price tag can feel a little steep. Hard-to-admit resentment against Jesus (and disdain for others) often lurks below the surface for rule-keepers.

Both groups need to grasp how the original Christmas Gift surpasses their stunted conceptions. A superb, invitingly brief handling of this is Tim Keller's *The Prodigal God: Recovering the Heart of the Christian Faith* (Dutton; also in a Penguin audio edition).

There's a reason this Manhattan pastor is a *New York Times* best-selling author. Time for only one book this January? Grab Keller.

JANUARY

(Bits & pieces for now into next year)

Lonely at Christmas? Or Wish You Could Be Alone?

Cords of wood for your soul's fireplace have been stacked by the wise, compassionate folks at the Christian Counseling & Educational Foundation. Their website (www.ccef.org) offers a shed-full of helpful page-turners, and more downloads than your iPod or Kindle can handle. You'll run across Jayne Clark's minibook *Single and Lonely*—good if your living room feels too quiet at Christmas. Timothy Lane's *Family Feuds: How to Respond* prepares you for difficult relatives at your doorstep, as does William Smith's little *How to Love Difficult People*. These titles can be read in thirty minutes, but you'll also find substantial logs to warm you for hours.

Yuletide Depression

For those suspecting that "Christmas" is Latin for "dark time," Dr. Ed Welch's *Depression: Looking Up from the Stubborn Darkness* (New Growth Press) is laced with understanding and warmth. From a skilled counselor who loves people who hurt.

My Kids Generous?

Each Christmas for many years, the Russell family of Birdsboro, Pennsylvania, piled into their car and morphed into the Surprise Package Company. Their creative outreach to the poor inspired the poem on pages 33–36. Guidance for your own family's Surprise Package Company, plus Roy Russell's ingenious "Four Quarter Method" for teaching children the wise use of money (including the joy of generosity), can be found at: www.SurprisePackageCompany.com.

How Jesus Helps on Monday Mornings

Andrée Seu Peterson writes a regular column in *World* magazine about her fears, early widowhood, finances, temptations, child-rearing woes, and the like—all with an invisible but very real Savior. She's brilliant, honest, and deep. Her "best of" articles are collected in *Won't Let You Go Unless You Bless Me* (about the size of this book), published by *World.* Several chapters have changed me permanently.

A Big City Story

At twenty-two, she packed their belongings, seat-buckled their daughter, and headed with her pastor-husband to one of Baltimore's most daunting urban neighborhoods. Their goal: to found an interracial church where the Savior's power to transform lives would be apparent.

The next twenty years—the cost, the fruit, how she herself changed—are movingly described in Maria Garriott's *A Thousand Resurrections* (Riott Publishing). Haunting. www.athousandresurrections.com. Maria's poems about her street, her adopted world, have appeared in numerous magazines and in *The Baltimore Sun*.

Proverbs

Solomon's tiny book deserves a tiny commentary. My favorite for years: Derek Kidner's wise and practical *The Proverbs: An Introduction and Commentary* (InterVarsity Press)—a pint of maple syrup boiled from sap-gallons of careful study in Hebrew. Dr. Kidner, an Anglican priest and one-time Warden of Tyndale House, Cambridge University, died at age 95 as I wrote *A Better December*. Thank you, good sir, for walking with Jesus for a lifetime.

Thanks to . . .

Agur, an otherwise-unknown ancient sage who penned Proverbs 30 (see pages 15, 51). For simplicity's sake, I subsumed his words under Solomon's. Who knows? Maybe Agur helped with Solomon's market research.

The Harmes family of Morgantown, Pennsylvania, whose lives of servanthood are a Mona Lisa to my scribbled portrait on pages 67–69.

Talented Brian Jackins (whose fingerprints touch each page). Creative Sarah Halulko (whose sketches are the real reason anyone will read this book). Our sacrificial church staff, who shore up all my weaknesses: Friend John Barber (without you I'd be in a padded cell). Kind Ginny Foltz, Deb Shirey, and Janet Albright. Brothers-in-the-trenches Matt Carter and Al Kimball. Selfless John Bell, for whom the verse was written, "The last shall be first." Wise Kathy Eberly, who endlessly inconveniences herself for me. Cheerful Andi Colmery and the front desk volunteers.

I must fess up. The kids on pages 21–22 were my Holly and Mark. Their grandmother was my mom. I'm pleased to report that Holly is still patting backs, and that Mark ("Age 24") is no longer a thumb-sucker.